The
Xenophobe's Guide to
The Germans

Stefan Zeidenitz
Ben Barkow

RAVETTE PUBLISHING

Published by Ravette Publishing Limited
P.O. Box 296
Horsham
West Sussex RH13 8FH
Telephone: (01403) 711443
Fax: (01403) 711554

First printed 1993
Reprinted 1994, 1995, 1996

Series Editor – Anne Tauté

Cover design – Jim Wire
Printer – Cox & Wyman Ltd.
Production – Oval Projects Ltd.

An Oval Project
for Ravette Publishing.

Contents

'While Germany is in this transition phase, Germans are suffering Angst like never before...'

The population of the reunified Germans is just short of 80 million: 63½ in the West and 16 in the East (compared with 48 million English, 57 million French, 57 million Italians, 7½ million Austrians, 8½ million Swedes and 6½ million Swiss).

Nationalism and Identity

Forewarned or Wurst Case Scenario

The prospect of the Germans may cause even the devoted xenophobe to break stride. Viewed by some as a nation of square-jawed robots whose language sounds like something awful in the drains, whose cars out-perform all others and whose football team seldom loses, the Germans seem unassailable.

But behind the façade lies a nation distinctly uncertain about where it is, where it is going, even how it got there. Seeking refuge from the world's uncertainties, on the one hand they rely on order and system, the State and the Bundesbank; on the other they retreat into the Angst of the soul, psychoanalysis and high culture.

None of this anxiety should be mocked; humour is a quite separate category to be viewed in a serious light.

For the Germans, life is made up of two halves: the public and the private. The public sphere of jobs, official-dom, business and bureaucracy is radically different from the private one of family, friends, hobbies and holidays. What is fitting in the one is quite impossible in the other. In public, po-faced propriety is the order of the day. In private, shell-suited eccentricity abounds.

As a foreigner you will, almost by definition, encounter public Germany first, and may never see more. This explains something of their reputation abroad. All those sausages, all that beer.

Now that German consolidation has become a reality, even non-xenophobes fear for the future. The Germans themselves are not so much fearful of foreigners as fearful of any foreign country getting a bad impression of the Germans. After all, their economy heavily depends on export markets.

How They See Others

The Germans generally adore the English and have suffered in the past from unrequited love. England used to be the ultimate role model with its amazingly advanced political, social, industrial and technological achievements. The Germans regard the English as being very nice and mostly harmless. Almost German.

The Germans admire Americans for their (un-German) easy-going pragmatism and dislike them for their (un-German) superficiality. For the Germans, the United States is the headmaster in the school of nations, and accorded due respect if not always affection.

The Germans have a close understanding with the Italians because they have so much history in common. Through wars, invasion and other forms of tourism, a deep and lasting friendship has been established. Italian art treasures, food and beaches are thoroughly appreciated.

There is also a connection arising from the fact that Italy and Germany both achieved nationhood in the last century, and are still not entirely sure that this was a good thing.

The French are admired for their sophisticated civilization, and pitied for their inferior culture. The French may have higher spirits, but the Germans have deeper souls. Despite this, Francophilia is widespread among Germans, especially those living close to the French border.

The Germans, like a wistful child looking over the garden fence, envy the Mediterranean people for their more relaxed attitudes, cultural heritage and warm climate, but only in the holidays.

The only people to whom the Germans readily concede unquestioned superiority of Teutonic virtues are the Swiss. No German would argue their supremacy in the fields of order, punctuality, diligence, cleanliness and thoroughness. They have never been to war with the Swiss.

If experience has taught them one thing, it is that there is no future outside the community of nations. No other nation has a stronger sense of the importance of getting along with others. Tolerance is not only a virtue, it is a duty.

How They See Themselves

Generally speaking, the Germans regard themselves as modest, rather ordinary sort of people. Give them a beer, a wurst, a bit of *Gemütlichkeit* (cosiness) and another German with whom to argue politics or bemoan the stress of life, and they will be content. They are not greedy, do not expect something for nothing, and pay their bills on time. Simple, honest *volk*.

The Germans like to dream, see themselves as romantic. Not in a Mediterranean flowery-compliments-and-bottom-pinching way, but in the stormy genius mode.

In every German there is a touch of the wild haired Beethoven striding through forests and weeping over a mountain sunset, grappling against impossible odds to express the inexpressible. This is the Great German Soul, prominent display of which is essential whenever Art, Feeling and Truth are under discussion.

The Germans did not actually invent the Romantic Movement (although they are pretty sure that they did), but they at least kitted it out with a lot of appropriately fraught and complicated philosophy.

They see themselves as profoundly well educated. Contrary to popular belief, the Germans do not know everything, they just know everything better.

Special Relationships

Before the 1990s all West Germans were passionately keen on the idea of the two Germanys coming together again. How, they asked themselves and each other, can we find fulfilment as a nation while the great German *Geist* (spirit) is divided by a concrete wall?

All were agreed that reunification was a historical necessity. The same sort of consensus never existed *drüben* (over there), where people generally coveted the consumer durables but had their doubts about life in a society without ideological commitments. Now that unification is a fact, West Germans have their doubts, too.

All Wessies (former West Germans) know that all Ossies (former East Germans) are idle and complaining. All Ossies know that all Wessies are cynical and deceitful. It was ever so.

Cementing two nations together doesn't come cheap, especially when one of them (in estate agent terminology) 'needs attention' and has many 'period details' and 'original features'.

In order to cope, the Germans set up The Trust Authority (*Treuhand*), which instantly became the world's largest employer, with 9,000 companies, nearly two million hectares of farm land and two million hectares of forest under its control. Its job is to privatise as much as it can, and shut down the rest.

Needless to say, the work of the Treuhand has created suspicion among eastern Germans, who feel that their economic assets are being sold at knock-down prices, while they are being treated as second class citizens. Tension between the two kinds of Germans is tangible.

While Germany is in this transition phase, Germans are suffering *Angst* like never before, and the soul-searching has taken on epic proportions. The effect has been to deepen German commitment to the ideals of the European Community still further; it offers a stable context for the turmoil within.

How Others See Them

The emotions which Germans arouse in others oscillate between admiration and fear – they are said to be either 'at your knees or at your throat'.

They are thought of as efficient, self-obsessed, arrogant and domineering – altogether too good at finance and manufacturing.

The English have always had a high regard for German cleverness and thoroughness, somehow imagining that of all Europeans, the Germans are most like themselves. This quaint illusion probably has its roots in the fact that so many Germans have occupied the British throne or been powers behind it.

The French regard the Germans with suspicion and a measure of loathing, and seek to contain them by chumming-up. The Italians are dumbfounded by the German capacity to get things done without bribing anyone, but regard them as utterly lacking in style.

To the Austrians, a good German is one who is far away – preferably across the Atlantic, or even further.

How They Would Like Others to See Them

The Germans long to be understood and liked by others, yet secretly take pride that this can never be. After all, how can outsiders understand such a complex, deep, sensitive people? What can they know of the German struggle for identity or the tortured German spirit searching for release?

The Germans would like to be respected for their devotion to truth and honesty. They are surprised that this is sometimes taken as tactlessness or worse. After all, if I know you to be in error, surely it is my duty to correct you? Surely the Truth is more important than pretending to like your ghastly shirt? Foreigners just cannot seem to appreciate this.

Dismissing German introspection as navel-gazing is taken as proof of shallowness. Complaints about German rudeness show misunderstanding. Germans console themselves that devotion to higher causes and being true to the demands of the inner self are bound to rub a few people up the wrong way. It is sad, but quite unalterable.

A good German wears his *Weltschmerz* (world-pain) on his sleeve and doesn't really mind being misunderstood.

Character

The Importance of Being *Ernsthaft*

In Germany, life is serious, and so is everything else. Outside Berlin, even humour is no laughing matter, and if you want to tell a joke you may want to submit a written application first.

The Germans strongly disapprove of the irrelevant, the flippant, the accidental. Serendipity is not a word in their language. The reason for this is that such things are not *Ernsthaft*, serious. It is hardly conceivable (and certainly not desirable) that a good idea might arise by chance or come from somebody lacking the proper qualifications. On the whole Germans would prefer to forego a clever invention rather than admit that creativity is a random and chaotic process.

Because life is *Ernsthaft*, the Germans go by the rules. Schiller wrote, 'obedience is the first duty', and no German has ever doubted it. This fits with their sense of order and duty. Germans hate breaking rules, which can make life difficult because, as a rule, everything not expressly permitted is prohibited. If you are allowed to smoke or walk on the grass, a sign will inform you of this.

In professional life, devotion to earnestness means that you cannot give up accountancy or computer engineering in mid-life and switch to butterfly farming or aromatherapy. Any such change of heart would cause you to be dismissed as lightweight and unreliable.

Order

The Germans pride themselves on their efficiency, organization, discipline, cleanliness and punctuality. These are all manifestations of *Ordnung* which doesn't just mean tidiness, but correctness, properness, appropriateness and a host of other good things. No phrase warms the heart of a German like '*alles in Ordnung*', meaning everything is alright, everything is as it should be. The categorical imperative which no German escapes is '*Ordnung muss sein*', Order Must Be.

Germans like things that work. This is fundamental. A car or a washing machine which breaks down six months after purchase is not a nuisance, it's a breach of the social contract.

They are mystified when they go abroad and see grimy buildings, littered streets, unwashed cars. On the platforms of the London underground they while away the hours between trains puzzling about why the crazy English put up with it and don't organize things properly. Even the language is unreliable and full of tricks, with people called 'Fanshaw' who spell their names Featherstonehaugh, and towns called Slough (of which you cannot get enough when passing through).

In Germany, they manage these things better. Words may be long and guttural, but there are no tricks to pronunciation – what you see is what you get. The streets are clean, the houses newly painted, the litter in the bins. *Ordnung*.

Angst

Predictably, in this immaculate garden lurks a serpent: doubt. As a nation the Germans are wracked with doubt and fight constantly to keep chaos at bay. Being German, they cannot brush their doubts aside or put off worrying in favour of a pint and a laugh.

Not for them the touching British faith that it 'will be alright on the night', that it 'all comes out in the wash'. For a German, doubt and anxiety expand and ramify the more you ponder them. They are astonished that things haven't gone to pot already, and are pretty certain that they soon will.

Germany is, after all, the Land of *Angst*.

It is said that this pervasive anxiety leads to a reluctance to undertake anything; that, when action is necessary, the Germans struggle with the difficulties.

Angst is responsible for their desire that everything be regulated, controlled, checked, checked again, supervised, insured, examined, documented. Secretly, they believe it takes a superior intelligence to realize just how dangerous life really is.

They see their anxiety as proportional to their intellectual capabilities.

Dream Inspired

The Germans enjoy escaping into fantasies whenever reality becomes too unpleasant. Failures and defeats require a metaphysical back-up system; they love to dream. The German equivalent of John Bull and Uncle Sam is sleepy-headed Michel, a name derived from Germany's patron saint, St Michael.

The poet Heinrich Heine summed up this propensity:

'The Frenchmen and Russians possess the land,
The British possess the sea,
But we have over the airy realm of dreams
Command indisputably.'

On occasion, the German fondness for escapism – their need for a spiritual essence, can make them seem other-worldly and impractical. Goethe noted wistfully, 'While we Germans torment ourselves with solving philosophical questions, the English with their practical intelligence laugh at us and conquer the world.'

Life's a Beach

The German craving for security is nowhere more evident than during holidays at the seaside. Here they have earned for themselves global notoriety for their ruthless efficiency in appropriating the best spots on the world's beaches.

No matter how early you struggle to get to the beach, the Germans will be there before you. Quite how they manage it remains a mystery, given that they can be seen carousing in the bars and tavernas until the small hours with the rest of us.

Having gained their beachheads, the Germans will immediately start digging in, constructing fortifications. You can always tell the beaches under German occupation: huge sandcastles cover the area, one per family, each several feet high, elaborately decorated with seashells and decaying starfish, crowned by flags.

Unlike everyone else, the Germans prefer to be inside their sandcastles, which then serve to mark out their territory – define their particular space. Often these structures are so tightly packed together there is no room left to walk between them.

In extreme cases non-Germans may find themselves sitting on bare rock, the Germans having excavated every grain of available sand for their Fortress Beachtowel.

Right to Wrong

You may on occasion be pulled up short by German bluntness and directness. The Germans are constitutionally unable to admit to being in the wrong or having made a mistake.

With their unshakable conviction that there is a right answer to everything, they have difficulty with shades of opinion. They will unhesitatingly express their disagreement in terms of your being wrong. Not, "I don't think you're right about that", but "That is false!"

If they don't like something, expect to be told so in no uncertain terms. Sparing other people's feelings is quite unnecessary since feelings are a private matter and have no business in public. While the English will engage in a form of agile verbal sparring, the Germans expect you to state your wishes clearly and directly, to use language at its face value. The Germans say what they mean and mean what they say:

"Do you know what time it is?"
"Yes, I do."

The Ideal

'Nobody is perfect, but we are working on it', said Baron von Richthofen optimistically. Perfectionism is a prime German characteristic which benefits their auto industry but can be a trial at parties. Compromise and settling for what is good enough is not good enough. Strictly speaking, only the ideal will do.

There is no doubt in the German mind that the ideal, or rather, the Ideal, exists and is out there somewhere in the ether. Naturally, here on earth, we can never achieve the Ideal, only a pale imitation of it. Plato may have been a Greek, but he thought like a German.

So it is not surprising that many Germans relate to ideas more than to people. As Goethe put it, 'The Experience is always a parody of the Idea'.

Ideas are beautiful and don't let you down; people are unpredictable and do. Clashes between ideas and reality are inevitable, and Germans are quite resigned to this. It is part of what makes life tragic.

This is reflected in German literature and legend. Many German heroes fall because they measure their ideals against the imperfection of their nature and that of the world. Lamenting this sad state of affairs is a German preoccupation. Making the best of a bad lot and taking the rough with the smooth are more or less alien concepts to the German mind.

Beliefs and Values

The Germans prize *Bildung*, meaning education and culture. Showing off what you've read and what you know is not gauche. It is a way of participating in the nation's cultural life and taking pride in it.

Modesty in regard to education will not be interpreted by them as hiding your light under a bushel, but as an admission of ignorance. If you've got it, flaunt it.

Germans have unequalled enthusiasm for their cultural heritage. For many English people, culture is what the advantaged do in their spare time, and the idea of reading Shakespeare or Samuel Johnson for fun is rather remote. For the average German this isn't so.

Not to have read the whole of Kant's *Critique of Pure*

Reason would surprise them (how could you allow yourself to miss out?), and they will have read Goethe and Schiller and Shakespeare with passionate, if uncritical, interest.

Being Green

The Germans worry about the environment. Green economics and green politics are much more developed than in England, where the Green Party has only slightly more credibility than Screaming Lord Sutch.

This particular preoccupation is founded on real concern. Industrial pollution is a major problem, much of it coming downstream in the Rhine, a river so full of chemicals that someone once managed to develop a photograph in water taken from it.

The state of many of western Germany's rivers is something of an own goal. Before reunification they exported most of their toxic wastes to East Germany, where a great deal was dumped unceremoniously into the nearest river, only to flow back into West Germany.

But what made the Germans really sit up and take notice was *Waldsterben*, the dying of the forests. The discovery that the economic miracle was killing their beloved forests gave the Germans a jolt they have yet to recover from.

Forests, even if seldom visited, exert a powerful influence on the Germans. They are regarded as the natural habitat which most shaped the German soul. It was from the forests that they emerged to rampage across Europe and lay waste to Rome 2000 years ago and it is to the forest that they return (in spirit at least) when modern life overwhelms them with its horrors and demands.

Even today, around 30% of the land is covered with

woodlands, and entering them gives the Germans a thrill of danger missing from their ordered urban life.

The German forests are primordial and awesome. Their crisis is a crisis for the German spirit.

The Germans are keen recyclers. There is no shortage of opportunity to sift their green bottles from their brown, their plastic from paper. At supermarkets, people can discard the packaging and leave it behind altogether. Manufacturers of white goods (fridges, ovens) nowadays make efforts to see that the parts and materials they use can be recovered and recycled.

Green concern and the commercialism that surrounds it leads to some absurd situations. The scrupulously separated waste is quite often thrown together again when it reaches the dump, and none of it recycled. And the demand for recycled paper is so great that the mills have to pulp perfectly good new paper to make it.

The Germans don't mind these imperfections in the system. Recycling is a beautiful idea, and that's what really counts.

Class

Germany does not have a class system any more. The old distinctive class differences have been levelled out since World War II. Nowadays nearly everybody belongs to the same class, which by English stratification could be roughly described as upper-lower-middle-middle class.

A small but significant number of German aristocrats does exist but, like their English counterparts they keep very much to themselves, hiding their wealth, land and influence with an un-German-like lack of show, many even sending their children to English boarding schools.

Not every 'von' denotes aristocracy; that of the so-called 'vegetable nobles' only means 'from', as in 'from the village of'.

German aristocratic titles correspond to the British ones in name only. Unlike the British tradition of leaving the title just to the eldest son, aristocrats in Germany pass on the parental title to all children. As Germany used to consist of of about 300 independent states, each with its own upper class, noble names have always been plentiful. Intermarriages with commoners can spread the name across all class barriers, especially since after a divorce the original commoner is entitled not only to keep the title, but to pass it on to future spouses and children as well, who will also...etc. This accounts for the astonishing abundance of titles in Germany today.

It is all part of a crafty scheme devised by the State to bring about such an inflation of nobility (at least in name) that eventually titles will become common and therefore meaningless.

Wealth and Success

On the whole, the Germans are not ostentatious in displaying their wealth. On the other hand, that massive gold jewellery makes a nice display and is ever so reassuring to have around. They appreciate quality, and are happy to pay for it. They are well-dressed, well-shod, drive solid cars, live in double-glazed and centrally heated homes equipped with lots of reliable gadgetry.

In Germany money tends to act as a social leveller. Living standards are higher than in Britain, and the consensus is that anyone who has earned it and can afford it deserves the best. There is little of the snobbery that insists people should 'know their place'. If your prosperity is the result of your labours or wit, few will dispute your right to enjoy it.

Religion

The Lutheran Church has had the greatest influence in shaping German attitudes. Luther's translation of the Bible shaped the modern German language, and it was part of his teaching that one's spiritual duties included obedience to worldly authority. In keeping with the Protestant work ethic, there is no very deep conflict between material well-being and one's prospects in the afterlife.

In Germany Protestants are in a slight majority (since reunification, which brought many East German Protestants into the fold). Broadly, the north is Protestant while the south is Catholic. The Catholic area coincidentally corresponds with the area under Roman occupation 2000 years ago.

Relations between the Churches are very good, with the spirit of ecumenicalism smiling benignly on all manifestations of religious life.

Churches are extremely well funded, the vast majority of the Germans gladly paying their church tax, even if most of them seldom turn up at services. This accounts for the presence of so many Mercedes in clerical garages, but also funds enormous amounts of welfare work.

At home, hospitals, kindergartens, old peoples' homes and schools are supported by church money. Abroad, money is channelled into famine relief and Third World Aid. The Germans have the best record in Europe on this score. Their preference is for steady, organized generosity rather than compassion binges of the Band Aid sort.

Behaviour

The Family

The Germans are family orientated, though not conspicuously more so than their neighbours. The family is the ideal, the focus for *Treue* (loyalty), but divorce rates are high, as couples succumb to the ubiquitous stresses of modern life.

German society as a whole is not well disposed towards children. In public your dog will usually get a warmer welcome than your offspring. Children are regarded as noisy and disruptive, liable to interfere with other people's right to quiet and *Ordnung*. Some of this may be explained by the fact that more Germans live in flats than houses, where noise and disturbance can be more problematic. Yet in the home, family life is warm, affectionate and *gemütlich* (cosy).

For the Germans, the concept of cosiness is much more than comfort. It is interwoven with the idea of *Heimat* – the cosy heart and hearth of home and family, the safeguard against *Angst* and homesickness, the warm and orderly shelter in a cold and chaotic world.

Eccentrics

The Germans do not share the English taste for public displays of eccentricity. This need surprise no-one in a country where neighbours have been known to complain about the irregular way others peg their washing out on the line (and have even rearranged it in a more pleasing symmetry).

Fitting in is a virtue, standing out an offence. As a foreigner, should you don a Union Jack waistcoat and kiss-me-quick hat, pedal around on a tricycle bedecked in pennants, and carry a selection of your favourite mice in your pocket, the Germans will assume that you're bonkers but will smile indulgently. Similar behaviour in another German will have them tutting furiously, looking up the number of the asylum, and worrying about the effect on property values.

The Elderly

The Germans also differ from the British on the matter of the elderly. This is an old person's society. Germans only really come into their own after retirement, at which point they discover within themselves reserves of conservativeness and a passion for *Ordnung* they had never dreamed of in their crazy youth.

To the average German senior citizen (and that is the only kind there is), life is a perpetual round of vigilantly seeking out infractions of rules and regulations, and helpfully (and loudly) pointing them out to the miscreants concerned.

In Germany, the autumn of life is the most *Ernsthaft* time of all, and you will never see a senior citizen smile or laugh in a public place (though they may permit themselves a wry chuckle in the privacy of their homes).

Other Germans treat the elderly with the deference and respect due them and eagerly anticipate taking their place among this élite.

Animals

The Germans are fond of their pets, which come in two forms – Alsatians, and preposterously small poodles wearing little woolly jackets and ribbons in their hair.

22

The point of these creatures is to be Obedient and Loyal (Alsatians) or to eat expensive chocolates and pooh everywhere (poohdles). Saying anything rude (or even mildly critical) to a German about his dog is more than your life is worth. All dogs are beautiful, and the world is their litter tray.

Those Germans who do not own a dog are strange (and could even be eccentric). Those who own a cat are certainly Communists and may be cut dead in the street. If the man next door acquires a budgerigar or hamster, any self-respecting German will think about moving house (and perhaps going to another town altogether).

Immigrants

Unlike America or, to a lesser extent, Britain, Germany is not a melting pot where peoples from diverse cultures are thrown together to make the best and worst of it. Remarkably few people immigrate in the true meaning of the word, to make their permanent home in Germany and to take up citizenship.

Foreign workers in Germany all intend to go 'home' eventually, even if they stay for decades. They live in a sort of mental and cultural limbo, not wanting to carve out a place for themselves in German society, and not really expected to. Their rootlessness is caught in the German word which describes them – *Gastarbeiter,* guest-worker.

German treatment of minorities will always be scrutinised by the outside world. Encouragingly, the majority of young Germans are passionate about supporting minority rights and wanting a multi-cultural society.

Violent exceptions to the general rule of indifference or goodwill are bound to grab headlines. In fact, for every act of hostility, there are many acts of kindness.

The guests were invited, they do the jobs which Germans don't want, they have brought a degree of internationalism to a parochial society and have worked wonders for German health, bringing urgently-needed relief from the national diet of unremitting stodge.

The largest group is the three million Turks, many of whose young are now of the third generation. The problems they face are repeated in most European countries. (Other groups of guest-workers include the Spanish, Italians, and Greeks who are regarded as co-Europeans.)

The Germans now face a different problem. Thousands of Poles, Romanians, Kurds, and other economic and political asylum seekers clamour to be allowed to live and work in Germany. The Ossie guards who used to be employed to keep people in, have had to be reassigned to patrol the Eastern borders to keep people out.

Why do the Germans envy the Chinese? Because they still have their Wall.

Manners

German manners are somewhat on the robust side. Don't expect an apology if somebody knocks into you on the pavement; what you'll get is a withering look for having had the selfishness and inconsideration to get in the way.

The withering look, a German speciality which you can observe children practising even in *Kindergarten*, is frequently accompanied by a muttered remark questioning the state of your mental well being. It is a German quirk that these remarks are always couched in the formal '*Sie*', never in the informal '*du*'.

Even when he or she has elbowed you out of the way, trodden on your feet, glared at you and is calling you a moron without the sense of a dead dachshund, a German will always address you as '*Sie*'. It would be unforgivably rude to do otherwise.

Queuing

The Germans are not great ones for queuing. At bus stops they won't entertain the idea on principle. It doesn't make the bus go any faster, and it doesn't help you get a seat, since this is down to the efficient use of elbows and withering looks.

In supermarkets they will queue, but grudgingly and only because there isn't any choice. In other shops, it is a matter of fine judgement. Queue-jumping might cause unpleasantness if the person you're planning to displace is in a hurry or pushing a pram or over sixty, but otherwise it's open season.

This rather chaotic approach seems out of keeping with the demands of *Ordnung*. And so it is. It appears that because shops and bus stops occupy an ambiguous position in the public/private divide, they are felt to present opportunities for free expression of the self. In the works canteen, the queue will have military precision.

Greetings

The Germans will shake hands at the drop of a hat. Hand-shaking is an unavoidable fact of life, and you will do well to reconcile yourself to pumping the flesh on all occasions. You must shake hands on meeting, on parting, on arriving, on leaving, on agreeing something, and on agreeing to disagree.

The Germans believe in the firm handshake which, done properly, should dislocate at least half a dozen of the smaller bones. It is considered a sign of friendliness to hold the hand for extended periods. If someone is crushing your hand in a vice-like grip and won't let go even as stars dance before your eyes and you feel your life-blood ebb, this simply means that they like you.

On the telephone, the Germans normally answer by stating their names. It's a nominal substitution for hand-shaking.

Formal and Informal: Sie-ing and Du-ing

The formal rules of etiquette are simple. When meeting someone for the first time, address them as '*Sie*' and continue to do so until the informal '*du*' becomes absolutely unavoidable (for example while sharing the post-coital cigarette and enquiring politely about earth-movements, etc.). A general guideline is that when you move on to first name terms, '*du*' becomes appropriate.

Social context will offer guidance: in business, never deviate from the formal. The Germans will remain on '*Sie*' terms with colleagues even after decades of sharing an office, and a boss calling his secretary by her first name will be universally suspected of having an affair with her.

In other contexts, informality may be the rule: when attending radical student functions, go for '*du*' even with perfect strangers to avoid accusations of bourgeois reaction.

German reluctance to move on to the informal level reflects how *Ernsthaft* a matter friendship is. Some

Germans accomplish the transition by stages.

To begin with, you will of course be addressed as Herr or Frau X. Later, should you discover sporting or other interests in common, and perhaps a mutual acquaintance or two, you may be addressed by your full name: 'So, Frank/Francine Jenkins, I am very pleased to see you once more...' Finally, after many months or years, you will move to first name terms, and '*du*' will ensue.

A variation on this, which should not cause alarm, is if you are called exclusively by your surname, 'Ach Jenkins, my old *Freund*!' It is essentially the same thing.

A distinct difference between English and German social life is the absence of petty hypocrisy. It is not good form to pretend to like someone for the sake of making a sale or gaining an advantage.

The strict separation of the public from the private provides a guarantee that in private the Germans are open and sincere.

They may lack polite cushioning phrases, seeing them as a waste of language, and keep their distance from strangers and acquaintances much longer than the English, but when you cross the Hellespont of the '*du*' it means that all reservations are gone and you have made a friend for life.

Obsessions

The Germans are obsessed with many things: it is a form of recreation among them. The state of their own health and that of society are favourite topics for dwelling on, at length. Both, they are convinced, are on the point of irreparable breakdown.

Simply look at the front covers of the news weekly *Der Spiegel* for an update on the latest versions of these twin obsessions. 'Is Impotence on the Increase?', 'What's Going Wrong With Germany?', 'Death of the German Novel?' are typical cover stories. Inside they will be dealt with in depth, with many an opinion by experts (no self-respecting German has confidence in anyone but an expert).

After 10 to 15 pages of minute analysis these articles come to no very firm conclusion beyond the certainty that things will go downhill from here on.

You may come to feel that the Germans are constantly in a state of crisis, and you'd be right. German life is a permanent emergency, teetering on the brink of the unthinkable. Crisis is its life's blood.

Cars

A further obsession is their cars. The Germans love their cars more than almost anything. While the Italians reserve this kind of adoration for their children, Germans prefer to keep their children indoors, so the cars can play safely in the streets.

German cars are pampered, primped and squeaky clean. Only a real brute with no feeling at all (or a foreigner) would drive around in an unwashed car. Such a person could be sure of disapproving glances and withering looks wherever he went.

Germans don't just derive status from their cars, they take their whole sense of identity from them. Cars are not a matter of life and death for Germans, they're much more important than that.

An Opel person is looked down on by a BMW person,

while Porsche people may be suspected of being flashy fly-by-nights. Naturally, the stately, solid, dignified Mercedes rules the roost, carrying its costly cargos of Herr Doktors and Herr Professors and Herr Direktors the length and breadth of the Republic.

Without doubt your car says more about you than cash ever could, and acts a bit like a sign of the zodiac, embodying character traits and distinctive features which mysteriously transmigrate to the person behind the wheel.

Even great historical events are symbolized and encapsulated in car lore. The collapse of Communism will be forever linked in the German mind with the Trabants (universally known as the Trabis), which came spewing through chinks in the Wall as fast as they opened up.

This sad little vehicle, like a blender on wheels, seems to embody everything that was wrong with the old GDR. Its two-stroke engine gushing pollution and generating virtually no horse power is a potent metaphor for the Eastern economy and industrial base. The tiny shapeless body perfectly represents the grey uniformity and undifferentiated social structures of the failed socialist state. No space, no status, and precious little *Technik* with which to get the ever-desirable *Vorsprung*.

Germans are utterly perplexed by the fondness which the British and other nations show for this little clockwork menace. No German would buy one, or hang on to it longer than he had to. While many a classic car collector might want one, because there will certainly be no other car like it, for the Germans it belongs on history's scrap-heap, along with every other reminder of the so-called Democratic Republic.

Leisure and Pleasure

Leisure is a bit of a problem for most Germans because by definition it consists of no-one telling you what to do or letting you know if you are doing it properly. In order to cope, the Germans do what they are best at: they make work out of it. Watching a German relax is terribly tiring, and makes you want to put your feet up for a while.

You will never see a group of Germans simply lounging around the park catching the rays of a summer's day. Leisure time is an Opportunity for Improvement, so on Monday mornings expect to hear detailed accounts of how the classes in Old Icelandic are going, or what went on at the Motormechanics for Mothers self-help workshop at the weekend.

Sport

Sport is the perfect excuse for working all day Saturday and Sunday. The Germans do not really see sport as a means of character-building. In a highly competitive society, sport is a popular way to improve and display one's general fitness and performance in an organized fashion.

Every third German citizen belongs to a sports club. Football, also the main spectator sport, is a traditional passion, while tennis became an overnight success after Wimbledon 1985. Boris and Steffi are seen as national heroes and adored for their effortful superiority.

Clubs

The Germans love clubs. It is said that whenever three Germans come together they will find some reason to form one.

If you see a group of Germans on a street corner, they're sure to be on a club outing of some sort. Clubs abound: there are well over 10,000 choral societies nationwide, and all other interests are represented in comparable numbers. Many have deep historical roots, as with the rifle and hunting clubs. Some of these date from the Middle Ages, and are swathed in guild-like ritual and tradition.

Clubbiness reflects the German dislike for doing things by themselves. Part of this is that they love organizing things. Frequently, the fun of being in a club is more to organize an activity than actually to carry it out. Every German's heart beats a little quicker at the thought of club business: committees, sub-committees, draft proposals, preliminary budget plans.

They love the opportunities for establishing status and doing a bit of social climbing. What nicer than being elected Club Secretary, Treasurer, vice-Chairman, Chairman. All this is done in a spirit of great seriousness, and with the utmost conscientiousness. And if once in a while you have to go on a country ramble or do rock climbing or whatever, well, it's a price worth paying.

Clubbiness begins early. Since few schools organize sports, most of the facilities and training are available only through clubs. The habit is acquired early and lasts through life.

It is by no means unheard of for someone to be buried with the insignia of their bowling or angling club, rather as certain football fanatics will name their hapless children after the entire team.

A uniquely German kind of club is the student fraternity. These are fundamentally drinking and duelling clubs but, being made up of typical males, everything is surrounded with all sorts of elaborate puff and ritual, including mottos and monograms, coloured ribbons and initiation rites, and the singing of drinking songs.

The classic image of the German aristocrat with a monocle screwed into his heavily scarred face owes its existence to the preposterous goings on in the student fraternities. Duels with sharp-bladed sabres are still fought as a test of courage.

One of the chief functions of clubs is to exclude others and offer identity and coherence to a group of people who otherwise may have little in common.

A club also serves to lend a measure of dignity to whatever the members get up to. A lone Morris dancer may encounter laughter and ridicule, a group of twenty will meet with more respect.

A characteristically clubby phrase has it that '*hier sind wir unter uns*' (Here we are among ourselves), a signal that you may let your hair down and enjoy yourself.

Sex

The Germans are as fond of sex as everyone else and remarkably tolerant of other people's foibles and peculiarities. There is great openness about sex – in-depth discussions about its problematic nature are inevitable wherever you go and any sign of embarrassment will be taken as a symptom of psychological hang-ups.

Seduction techniques leave something to be desired, and many Germans seem to rely on the age old method of boring the pants off you.

Once under way, expect full-blooded and vocal expressions of pleasure and delight (or disappointment), and don't be taken aback by frank comparisons of technique, duration, etc.

The commercial face of sex is coarse, vulgar and occasionally very strange indeed. For details, see Hamburg's Reeperbahn. In general, licensed premises and persons receive routine health inspections thus reducing the risk of contracting any unpleasant surprises.

However, if you like your sex to be a mysterious smouldering ecstasy, choose the French. To the Germans it is more like an invigorating work-out in the gym or, in extreme cases, minor surgery.

Sense of Humour

The Germans take their humour very seriously.

Harsh, astringent and satirical is their style. The cabarets of pre-war Berlin are famous. Their bite was ferocious: the English *Spitting Image* is playful by comparison. Classic German satire put the boot in and twisted the knife.

Surprisingly the tradition of political satire was kept alive in East Germany, where most major cities had their state-run cabarets. Scripts were vetted by the authorities, jokes at the expense of the West encouraged, and some barbed observations about life at home permitted. The comics' propensity to ad-lib gave spice to the entertainment, because they might at any moment say something 'dangerous'.

The Germans also have a strong sense of the ridiculous and silly, and a healthy appreciation of the way life can ruin the best laid plans. The operation of Sod's Law will usually occasion a wry smile and a dry remark.

German humour does not translate very well. While the Germans can understand British humour because most speak English, most German jokes when translated into English are no funnier than the average till receipt. Learn a bit of German, and you'll soon come to realize that there is a rich seam of humour running through German life.

But their humour is largely a matter of context. There is a time and a place for being funny and for laughing. *Ordnung* decrees that humour is not the oil that makes the days run smoothly.

You do not tell jokes to your boss (although levity with other colleagues may be all right at times), nor do you lard your sales pitch or lecture with witticisms. Irony is not a strong German suit and may easily be misunderstood as sarcasm and mockery.

German humour tends to have a target. While the Germans are happy to laugh at others, and especially the misfortunes of others (other Germans, that is), their faltering self-confidence doesn't allow for self-ridicule.

The Germans do not joke about foreigners; jokes about East Germans only began *after* reunification.

The butt end of their humour centres on regional characteristics: the stiffness of the Prussians, the brash, easy-going nature of the Bavarians; the bovine East Friesians, the quickness of Berliners, the slyness of the Saxons.

The Bavarians see jokes as a convenient way of taking revenge on their old archenemies, the Prussians. The Swabians don't mind jokes about their thriftiness, but prefer to be economical with them. Hence:

A Prussian, a Bavarian and a Swabian are sitting together drinking beer. A fly falls into each one's mug. The Prussian pours away his beer with the fly and orders a new beer. The Bavarian picks the fly out of his mug with his fingers and continues drinking. The Swabian picks out the fly and then forces it to spit out the beer it has drunk.

Humour in Germany is also subject to an official timetable. A good example is the custom of the *Karneval* celebration which is particularly popular in the Rhineland. It starts officially at 11 minutes past 11 o'clock on November 11th (no insult to Remembrance Day intended here, it just happens that 11.11 is a very orderly numerical combination to the Germans, and order is also pivotal to emotional enjoyment).

Pageants, parties and performances continue for some months, all with the official obligation to be funny. To avoid disorder, strict rules have been set up to organize the merriment as efficiently as possible. During congregational speeches, which are endless concoctions of jokes, every joke is marked by an orchestral signal so that nobody will laugh at the wrong moment.

Disorderly humour is not only nothing to laugh about, it is often not even recognised.

Culture

German culture is for the most part earnest, and big. Not for them the slender volume of elegant stories beloved of the French. Nor do they like the wry observations of village life or frail metaphysical puzzlings of the contemporary English novel. Germans want value from their *Kultur* and *Kunst*, and value means bulk.

No would-be cultural icon can get away with a small oeuvre. Just look at what they're up against: Collected Works of Goethe, 143 volumes – even workaday selections will weigh in at anywhere between 15-50 volumes; Collected Works of Nietzsche, 30 volumes at least; Wagner's operas, two weeks listening if you don't break for meals or sleep; *Heimat* and *Heimat II*, as long and convoluted as life itself.

It is perhaps because paintings can't be long that the Germans have never really gone in for this form of expression. But Buildings are quite big, and you may expect excellent architecture, old and contemporary.

The trick when confronted by all this massiveness is not to be intimidated. Break off a manageable chunk. Suck it and see. You will be pleasantly surprised – at times, astonished.

German culture in general and literature in particular is different from others in two main ways: it is comparatively young, having only really got going during the 18th century, and it is highly self-conscious with characters in plays even from the 19th century stepping out of the framework of the drama to complain to the author or argue points with members of the audience.

It arose in response to a powerful sense of inferiority that there was no body of specifically German art, and a creeping *Angst* that other nations might regard the Germans as philistine.

The man who changed all this, and who dominates German culture like a colossus, is Goethe. Almost single-handedly he gave Germany a literature to be proud of, comparable with anything the French, the English or the Italians can offer. He put the Germans up there with the best of them, where they have ever longed to be. He seemed to contain the entire German *Seele* (soul) within him, and for this he is cherished, loved, adored.

Ponderous German scholarship has almost hidden him from view. This is a shame, because there never was a livelier, more fascinating writer.

He brims and fizzes and bursts with energy and ideas. His intellect soars with the exuberance of a champagne cork in flight. He contributed new and extraordinary things in poetry, novels, drama, travel writing, autobiography. With something to say about everything, his ideas range from the dazzling to the downright daft.

In his youth, Goethe was a star without parallel, the Michael Jackson of his day. When he dressed a character in his first novel in blue and yellow and had him commit suicide for unrequited love, Europe's youth donned blue and yellow and penned tragic farewells.

In old age he was the grandest of old men, and all his conversations were taken down verbatim. Hardly a day of his life is unaccounted for, hour by hour (i.e. 'Goethe: The Missing Twenty Minutes').

Goethe is the German Shakespeare, and Shakespeare, too, is a sort of honorary German thanks to the classic translation by A.W. Schlegel and L. Tieck. '*Sein oder nicht sein*' (To be or not to be) echoes around many a packed house, and lots of Germans think of Shakespeare as a German who simply lived in the wrong place.

On the whole, it is not recommended that you come to German literature looking for a happy ending. You won't find one. Happy endings are not soulful and certainly not serious.

Germans love philosophy every bit as much as they love literature. *Dichter und Denker* runs the phrase, meaning Poets and Thinkers, cultural heroes both. The philosophers to crib quotes from include Fichte, Hegel, Kant, Leibniz, Nietzsche, and Schopenhauer – heavyweights besides which French or English philosophers can only be awarded a contemptuous sneer.

German art (*Kunst*) is introspective, brooding, self-obsessed; in a word, German. The message is more important than the medium; heavily indigestible (but brilliant) ideas. The core is what matters, not the outward shell.

The '50s and '60s saw an outpouring of plays and novels chronicling the *Angst* Germans felt in relation to their unresolved past and in the face of the material success, but spiritual emptiness, of contemporary society. In Britain, these had their counterpart in Angry Young Men.

Political themes also came to the fore, with some of the best writing coming from East Germany. Many of these writers opted to escape to the West; those that remained at home risked accusations of collaboration with the East German secret police.

The Germans need a small, restricted, clearly defined area of chaos to offset their sense of order. The cinema offers it.

After the work of directors like Fritz Lang and Leni Riefenstahl, the emergence of a new and radical cinema rather startled everyone. Fassbinder, Herzog, Schlöndorf, Margarethe von Trotta, Wim Wenders and others have produced a series of extraordinary, bleak, bizarre and intense films which deal with German themes, or wider ones in a uniquely German way.

They might be tough to sit through, but they pass the test of being *Ernsthaft* with flying colours.

Television

German television is lamentable. The staple diet is dire imports from the U.S. and Europe, dubbed with ham-fisted insensitivity. It comes as quite a shock to see your favourite drama serial in Germany, the characters growl and squeak in a variety of unlikely voices you wouldn't have dreamt up for them in a hundred years.

German continuity announcers are inhumanly silken-voiced and slick. You will be continually addressed as 'Ladies and Gentlemen' and 'Honoured Viewers', and the evening will pass with a series of chiming noises and strange pauses during which nothing happens.

Programming for children is among the best in Europe, so adult taste for old fashioned items is a surprise. There are times when you simply cannot escape the welter of black and white minstrels, barber shop singers, and pseudo glamourous circus-style big band shows.

Comedy is popular, and though sitcoms are not what they're best at, imports go down well. News programmes and documentaries are long, in-depth and wearyingly stuffed with politically balanced expert analysis.

German television has always been responsive to the needs and wishes of the young. Even in the early '70s, German youth had access to far superior popular music shows, where they could see and hear not just banal chart favourites, but cult 'underground' acts like the Grateful Dead, Velvet Underground and the other exotic oddities of the era.

Perhaps this is because any manifestation of culture, no matter how awful, might turn out to be 'important', in which case to have ignored it would be philistine. Better cover it, just in case.

The Press

The Germans are great believers in press freedom. Over 300 daily newspapers jostle in the marketplace, although naturally a handful dominate.

Most of the titles are regional, with small circulations. The only truly national titles are *Die Welt*, *Bild*, and *Frankfurter Allgemeine*. *Bild* is a mass-circulation scandal sheet along the lines of *The Sun*, only more so ('Girlfriend Beheaded, Cooked and Tinned in 39 Pieces!'); lighter problems, like world recession, are covered by the other two, with the *Frankfurter Allgemeine* roughly filling the niche occupied by the *Financial Times*.

Conversation and Gestures

'Small-talk' is an expression which has no direct equivalent in German. People would be mortified at the suggestion that any utterance they make is less than portentous.

The English compulsion for discussing the weather is looked on with wry compassion. Instead the Germans are delighted to discuss the enormous strain and pressure of their work, hardships, stress symptoms, illnesses, doomsday and other uplifting topics.

Other popular themes are holidays and how much you need one, how much you had to work last week, why you really need a holiday now, why you have to work even harder this week and how to interpret holidays and work in terms of Planck's quantum theory, Hegel's idea of the absolute or the new tax reform – topics which should be approached with the utmost circumspection, lest you are suspected of being sarcastic or lightweight.

The polite English 'How are you?' is likely to be answered with a comprehensive, head-to-toe survey, taking in all the bodily systems and missing none of the major organs. If you don't want to know, you'd do well not to ask.

Insults

The Germans dearly love to swear and curse, and have any number of explosive epithets with which to do it.

Bodily functions are graphically referred to whenever anything goes wrong. *Scheiße* (shit) is used so frequently and by so many people that many Germans are not even aware that it is a swear word.

The legal consequences of verbally insulting another

person can be severe. Gross mutilation or disablement of a crime or accident victim receive small financial compensation, but hefty fines result from publicly questioning somebody's intelligence, such as pointing at your forehead – the derogatory gesture popular with motorists that suggests someone has taken leave of their senses. The Germans take care not to indulge in trading insults in the presence of the police.

The middle finger raised is equivalent to the English 'V' sign, and three fingers extended to form a 'W' used by neo-Nazis is strictly prohibited (as is any Nazi symbol, the salute or the swastika – even on a toy model of a Messerschmitt).

The gesture most frequently displayed is the raised index finger. In every German there lurks a lecturer, longing to get out.

Custom and Tradition

The Germans value customs and follow them assiduously. They love traditions and have plenty of them though the majority of them are of local rather than national origin.

Most are a more or less elaborate ritual preparation for the consumption of enormous amounts of beer.

Many customs and traditions are linked with the ubiquitous clubs. Rifle clubs, *Trachtenvereine* (clubs for the wearing of local traditional costumes), pigeon fanciers clubs all have their festivals which may typically consist of beer drinking, a religious ceremony, beer drinking, a parade, beer drinking, and be rounded off nicely with a glass or two of beer.

For the ceremony of *Richtfest* (roof-topping), which

marks the completion of the roof timbers before the slates go down, a party is given by the house-owners for their friends and neighbours, and the builders. Much beer is consumed. Finally, a beribboned wreath or small tree is fixed to the summit of the roof, to let everyone know that the work is going well and that the owners have done the right thing.

The business of wine-making and brewing and harvest time brings festivals to celebrate nature's bounty. The greatest of these, the Munich Beer Festival, *Oktoberfest*, is famous the world over. Over 16 days, locals and visitors down enough pints to keep a small country going all year, and make a serious dent in the chicken population.

To keep them in the mood, there is much jovial arm-linking and singing of boomps-a-daisy German songs while swaying to and fro hoping not to fall over just yet. If you have ever longed to dress up in lederhosen and tunic or dirndl and frilly bodices, and bob about in a tide of large bosoms and bellies, the *Oktoberfest* is for you.

The majority of customs and traditions are linked to the Christian calendar. Notable are the celebrations before Lent. These have their origin in ancient fertility ceremonies to welcome the returning spring, and retain their pagan character. They usually feature some variation on the carnival Prince, Princess and Peasant (always men, even the Princess) who are the presiding spirits of madness.

During the 'Crazy Days' of Karneval, *Ordnung* goes out the window and the entire ethos of German worka-day life is turned upside down. But on Ash Wednesday, everyone is back at work in a very *Ernsthaft* mood indeed, ready to knuckle under for another year, yet cherishing their memories of the mayhem.

Christmas

Christmas is the main focus for tradition and custom, and is every German's favourite time of year. The British Christmas is a pale and thin imitation, which owes what little *Gemütlichkeit* it has to the efforts of Prince Albert to bring a little cheer to the benighted country he was married into.

Advent is marked by decorating the front door with a wreath. Indoors the children are given an Advent calendar, so they can enjoy the count-down by opening a little door each day to see some Christmassy picture or find a little sweet. On the mantelpiece or dining table, another wreath will have four candles on it for lighting on the Sundays, first one, then two and so on until all four are lit the Sunday before the big day.

St. Nikolaus Day is celebrated on December 6, a sort of dry-run for Christmas. Children are required to put a shoe outside their bedroom door the night before, which is then filled with goodies while they sleep – provided their behaviour during the year has merited it.

In the run-up to Christmas, most towns have a Christmas market in the town square or outside its main church. Here you can find all manner of cheap and cheerful trinkets for sale as well as spiced cakes, punch and seasonal sweet treats, a funfair and Christmas carols played by musicians in the church spire or some other conspicuous place.

The distribution of the presents is a rather formal event on Christmas Eve. Children are banished from the house (or at least kept out of the living room) in the afternoon, while the tree is set up and decorated. Tradition requires a dinner of carp, but this is generally held to be so unpalatable that most people opt for roast turkey, goose, venison (or sausages) instead.

Eating

German food has a poor reputation, being held to consist of fat and carbohydrates and very little else. It has been said that to the French the quality of food matters, to the Germans the quantity, while the English are concerned with nothing but table manners.

The Germans do not scoff constantly, but once their eating gains momentum it's hard to stop. Overdoing it is a German habit, and not only where food is concerned.

Part of the German reputation for greed stems from the fact that before, during and immediately after the War food was scarce and poverty was rife, so that meals were monotonous and small.

As food returned to the shops and cash to the wallets, the Germans embarked on an orgy-gorgy of epic proportions. This became known as the *Fresswelle*, a tidal wave of face-filling over-indulgence which produced the quadruple chinned generation who constitute the very stereotype of the German physique.

Eventually the Germans came to terms with the coronary consequences of their less than delicate eating habits. Where once they ate about three times as many potatoes as the British, they now eat twice as much health-giving fruit and fibre-rich veg. Today, the label 'light' is a sure-fire sales booster as the Germans determine to avoid ending up like their barrel-shaped elders. There are even 'light' mineral waters boasting less carbon dioxide.

One preference is unabated. Germans eat more pork than any other European country, four and a half million tons of it a year, or the equivalent of 5½ ounces of pork per person per day. The Germans have an old saying: 'One cannot live from bread alone, there must be sausage and ham as well.'

The German breakfast will feature orange juice, fresh coffee (not instant, *dankeschön*), a choice of bread with a selection of jams for the sweet-toothed and hams, salamis and cheeses for those requiring something a touch more substantial.

German bread comes in all shapes and sizes, and in a good many colours, too. In fact, about 200 different kinds of bread are available, and the Germans have a strong preference for the wholemeal (no health fad, this, they have always liked it that way). From rye bread to Pumpernickel, *Schwarzbrot* (black bread), to pretzels, German bread is a meal in itself.

Mid morning, the Germans like to snack so that they don't expire before lunch – the most substantial cooked meal of the day.

Mid afternoon requires you to stop what you're doing (unless you're at work) and go in search of 'coffee and cake'. The cakes will be enormously elaborate affairs layered with fruit, cream, chocolate, cream, sponge and extra cream.

Supper* is called *Abendbrot*, indicating that bread and cold cuts are again the order of the day, although cooked meals are common, too. Then before bed-time you may like to eat a little something just to keep night starvation at bay.

Of all the worries you have about Germany, the fear of going hungry has the least foundation.

---

*You may be surprised at the early hour (from 6.00-7.30 p.m.) at which Germans eat. No dinner at eight for them, let alone the Mediterranean habit of sleeping all afternoon and eating at midnight. Germans want to get it over with: they've got work to do.

Drinking

One in three of the world's breweries are in Germany. This alone should tell you what the Germans think about beer. Not so much a way of life, more the be-all and end-all of it.

In Germany small, local breweries manage to survive and thrive not just in ones and twos but in droves. Beer has a traditional association with monasteries, where much of it used to be brewed. It has been classed as a basic food, and even prescribed as medicinal (as stout still may be for the English – though prescription charges make this an expensive way of enjoying a Guinness).

One reason German beer is of such a high quality is the German Beer Purity Regulation, laid down in 1516 and unaltered since, which states that only water, hops, malt and yeast may go into beer. The only time the majority of Germans expressed serious doubts about being in the European Community was when the Eurocrats tried to tell them that this law had to go in the interests of regulatory 'harmonisation'. The Eurocrats soon backed down.

So while some 4,000 brands of pure German beer are offered, all imports are specially labelled to warn of their impure and contaminated state.

Beer is always served cold with a generous layer of foam. Such an orderly head can require up to eight minutes to be poured and is not recommended for thirsty drinkers in a hurry.

The most popular beer is 'Pils', which is also the number one export, in contrast to 'Export' beer which is hardly ever sent outside the country, and 'Alt' (old) beer which is drunk as young as possible.

German wines are excellent and, unlike the Californians who more often choose French over their own, are deeply appreciated by the Germans (although the French turn up their noses at them). Wine drinkers and beer drinkers are identical in Germany, there is no either-or.

Despite, or because of, being such a boozy lot, there is no toleration of drunkenness on the roads. Limits are lower than elsewhere, and penalties stiffer. Eat, drink, be merry – but take a taxi home.

Health and Hygiene

Virtually all Germans have health problems, and if they don't, there must be something wrong with them. Most of what ails them is stress related. No nation was ever more stressed, but this is understandable. After all, running Europe can take it out of you.

The delicacy of the German constitution has been long recognised, and smoothly-running systems put in place to bolster it and keep it going. In the 1880s Bismarck set up a national health insurance scheme. Today that national health insurance underpins a vast and wonderful network of doctors and hospitals, specialists and spas.

As with the French, the Germans devote enormous resources to the treatment of an illness which doesn't exist, in this case the notorious *Kreislaufstörung*, meaning disruption of the circulation. While the rest of us go to meet our maker once our circulation stops, the Germans routinely recover from it and go on to lead useful and productive lives. Once they are good at it, the Germans can have a *Kreislaufstörung* as often as twice a month without it seriously impairing their social life.

Treatment for this frightening disease varies. It has been shown to respond positively to three weeks on a Greek beach, and the prognosis isn't too bad if you take plenty of pills and potions. (It doesn't really matter what pills and potions, the secret lies in ostentatiously stopping work and lining up an awesome array of small brown bottles on your desk before swallowing six of everything and sighing copiously.)

Only one instance of someone actually dying because of *Kreislaufstörung* is recorded, a sad case of a young man whose pill-taking regime was so complicated that the schedule simply left no time for taking meals.

If *Kreislaufstörung* is an ailment which properly belongs in the realm of ideas, the main health worry for the Germans in the real world is the condition of their hearts. For the older generation who took part in the *Fresswelle* this was with very good reason. The veins and arteries of these lumbering, wobbling colossi were choked and begging for mercy. Thrombosis was an ever-present threat.

For their jogging-suited, water-sipping successors however, concern for the heart is less warranted and has taken on a hundred shades of metaphysical *Angst*.

Because all Germans pay 6.3% of their income into health insurance, and all contributions are matched by employers, German doctors are very pleased with life, and drive some of the newest and shiniest Mercedes on the roads. Dentists are so highly paid their main problem consists of finding sufficient deductible ways of spending to offset against their taxes.

In addition to six weeks' paid holiday, the Germans are entitled to a staggering six weeks' paid sick leave per year; and if you can fool them into it, the medical insurance companies will stump up for a further 78 weeks (over a 3-year period). All this costs a fortune – social security spending swallows about a third of Germany's gigantic GNP, and cutbacks are taking place, cautiously. Everybody in the government knows that it is safer to steal a lioness's cub than to come between a German and his medication.

Spas

A uniquely German institution is the spa cure. It is conclusive proof of earnestness and *Seelenhaftigkeit* (soulfulness) to recognise the need to repair body and mind, and shoot off to one of these spas at the State's expense at the first sign of a sniffle or an ingrowing toenail. Once there you will wallow in special curative muds and drink unspeakably foul waters, in between taking moderate exercise (i.e. walking to the cake shop and back) and playing the time-honoured game of How Much Schnaps Can I Sneak Before Herr Doktor Notices.

A curiosity of the regulations governing being sent on a *Kur* (cure) is that you are expressly forbidden to take your husband or wife, on the grounds, presumably, that you need rest and recuperation, not being nagged or having to submit to Unreasonable Demands. In Baden Baden, where the wealthy take their cure, the mixed sauna acts rather like a butcher's display, allowing you to inspect your bit of rump steak thoroughly before buying.

The consequence is known as the 'Spa Romance', from which patients and divorce lawyers both derive much solace.

Older lavatories in Germany have a curious ledge in the bowl. This puzzles and distresses many foreigners. What is it there for? The answer is the extraordinary curiosity of the Germans concerning everything to do with their health, and the fact that, should you spot some abnormality, it could provide the key to any number of weeks off work and a bit of slap and tickle at the *Kur*. Simple, really.

Hygiene

To the Germans, hygiene is the basic requirement of life and the absolute starting point of *Ordnung*. An unwashed German is a contradiction in terms, like a faithful Frenchman or a good English café.

In a German bathroom cabinet you will find a dazzling array of preparations and pieces of precision engineering for maintaining the human form in pristine condition. Dental hygiene takes pride of place. Only the very poorest of Germans will have one toothbrush, the remainder boast whole banks of them, with mirrors on sticks and high-speed water jets for persecuting every last molecule of plaque.

The tendency in modern homes is for each member of the family to have their own bathroom because the morning routine is so drawn out that sharing has become impossible; the last in line would simply never get out of the house.

Germans are passionately fond of every form of tonic and pep-me-up. They will swallow every conceivable kind of plant extract and animal gland, and will never doubt the good it is doing them, provided only that they have paid enough for it and that it tastes vile. It's all they ask.

What is Sold Where

On the whole, you will find German shops formal and a bit stuffy. The cheaper kind of department stores are an exception. They resemble a poorly organized jumble sale, and jumble sale rules apply, so wear shoulder pads and a protective helmet. Elsewhere the standard of decorum is such that you are expected to keep your end up by dressing smartly just to gain entrance.

The German-style chemist shop is the apothecary, a mysterious place where there is virtually nothing on display beyond perhaps some dentifrice or manicure equipment. Behind the spotless counter is the spotless white-coated apothecary, as *Ernsthaft* an individual as you'll meet anywhere, to whom you tell your woes and who, after some pretty close questioning, produces the sought-after box or bottle. Many of these shops are venerable and old, wood panelled and lined with marvellous glass or ceramic jars. They are a trifle intimidating with their sombre medicinal atmosphere but if you're feeling frail, a visit to the *Apotheke* will be balm to the soul.

Systems

The Germans appreciate a system. There's nothing quite like having a system, if you ask a German. Systems make the world go round.

Take their motorway system. Germany's autobahns came into existence because Hitler wanted to avoid his tanks and armoured vehicles getting stuck in traffic. He also had an unemployment problem to solve.

It seemed a good idea at the time, and proved its worth as a peacetime amenity. Getting around was easy and quick. Since then, getting around has become harder but that is due to the volume of traffic, not the roads.

The original autobahn system was an elegant one; in the former East Germany parts of it can still be seen in near-pristine condition, cobbled slip roads and all. Naturally, the Germans are working furiously to upgrade these old relics and prepare them for the road haulage avalanche which the development of a market economy will doubtless necessitate.

German law decrees that on the autobahn no speed limit applies, although there is a politely 'recommended' limit of 80 miles per hour to which only first-time visitors pay any attention.

To the Germans this unexpected freedom from restraint represents an important niche of liberty in an otherwise red-taped society. The freedom of the open road, the opportunity for self-expression by slamming down the hammer and leaving the rest standing, is cherished.

You can see the gleam in their eyes, and stuck fast in the sweltering tail-backs which characterise so many German roads around the big cities, you will have plenty of time to do so.

The Germans have some unique regulations governing filter lights. The only way of coping is never to place yourself at the head of any queue of traffic; then you can just do what the others do, safe in the knowledge that none of them is likely to bend, let alone break, any of the myriad codes of the road. (By law, cars must even be furnished with a pair of surgical gloves.)

If by some misfortune you do find yourself first in line at the lights, your best bet is to abandon your car there and then; it will be better than facing up to the barrage of hoots and roars of those behind you.

Public Transport

Your best bet is to go by bus or tram or train – every one of them a model system of efficiency and cleanliness.

The trains are fast, and punctual, partly because stations are sensibly placed in the centre of towns and cities. The intercity services are known as IC and the new intercity express service ICE is very fast, and features luxuries like fax machines, telephones and video.

In many of the cities confusion awaits you at the tube station. Do you take the 'U' Bahn or the 'S' Bahn? The 'U' Bahn goes underground while the 'S' Bahn goes overground. Except of course when it's the other way around. For maximum convenience, the 'S' Bahn seems to stop at most of the places where the 'U' Bahn does (though not the other way around, the 'S' Bahn reaching the parts other Bahns can't).

On certain stretches your 'S' Bahn ticket will cover you for travelling on the 'U' Bahn. On other stretches, it won't. Similarly, you may be covered for some bus routes and may even be able to take advantage of the excellent though dwindling tram service. But then again you may not.

Don't look for signs to explain it to you, there aren't any. Don't bother asking the ticket salesman even if there is one, the explanation will only baffle you more. Play it safe and buy whichever ticket includes everything, the extra expense is well worth it. Otherwise, walk.

Education

The German education system is not concerned with character-building or instilling moral fibre. Instead the aim is to load you with qualifications which will earn you respect and promotion in the market place.

Education for the Germans starts late and finishes even later. Nursery school is optional, primary school starts at the age of six, and the average student finishes university in his or her late twenties.

At ten years old the brighter pupils go to a *Gymnasium* (which is not for training the body but for training the mind) leading to university. The rest (some 60%) go to other secondary schools which are likely to take them towards an apprenticeship – a highly formalised 3 years in a shop, bank or whatever, including weekly theoretical training in a State run vocational school. For many this leads directly into a career.

Achieving the German *Abitur* (the final examination) automatically guarantees a place at university in almost any subject you like. If your average isn't good enough you may have to wait a few years, but rejection is not on the cards.

The Germans have to do National Service, being drafted as soon after their 18th birthday as school allows. You may object to military service and be given civilian service instead; but if flat feet or bad sight should exempt you, you are let off both. Some are even lucky enough to avoid either, if the year's intake is full.

Qualifications

Every German you encounter professionally will be thoroughly trained and qualified. Degrees are coveted. An academic degree is prestigious and must be prominently displayed. Still more desirable is a doctorate. Being entitled to style yourself '*Doktor*' lends power to your elbow in every sphere, be it business, finance, the law, even medicine. It is not thought in the least odd to call somebody 'Dr. Dr.' if they have two doctorates, and good manners require you to.

Top of the tree and most prized is the professorship. If you come up against someone called Herr Professor you know you are dealing with a true heavyweight. Professorships are usually hard to come by, requiring a lengthy, complicated thesis and giving weekly lectures (sometimes without pay) while waiting for a professorship which may never turn up.

Academic titles can of course be acquired with less effort by buying them, and this is regularly done by ambitious people in a hurry. Pretty much any title is available for a price if you know where to go (most commonly a third world country), and this form of aggrandisement is not illegal.

Money Matters

To the Germans money represents security. Fear of losing their beloved Mark prompted them to question the value of European unification. Of course sacrifices would have to be made, but preferably not on the financial front.

Twice this century, after the First and Second World Wars, Germany was hit by devaluation. Inflation reached astronomical proportions in the early 1920s. Everyone became a billionaire, yet money was not worth the paper it was printed on. The majority of Germans lost all their savings.

Even today, inflation is seen as the ultimate economic chaos, something to be restricted at all costs. The shock of it still lingers in the German soul.

Banks therefore play an even bigger part in business life than elsewhere. A system of 'universal' banking means that the banks own everything the government has not already got its hands on, while the *Bundesbank* (*Bundes* = Federal), as we all know, exists to guarantee the invincibility of the Deutschmark and ruin the economies of Europe.

Government

Germany is not only the Land of *Angst*, it is also the Land of the *Land*. Before reunification, there were 10 *Länder* (11 if you include Berlin), the NBLs (New Federal Lands) make it 15 (16).

Each *Land* is a politically separate region, with powers and responsibilities laid down by the Constitution, and each is represented in Bonn, in a rather ambassadorial manner, competing with the others to secure its interest at Federal level.

Federal Government is in charge of things like foreign policy, defence, taxes and telecommunications, while the *Länder* call the shots in the matter of education, policing, broadcasting and local government. Federal and *Land* governments go halves in splitting tax revenues, although by law no *Land* is allowed to become significantly richer or poorer than another. If they do, they have to hand it over.

The *Bundestag* is the highest law-making body. It elects the Chancellor (equivalent to the Prime Minister) who is the leader of the party with the largest number of seats, and safeguards democracy by allowing minority groups the right to demand information and ask for committees of enquiry into any funny business.

The *Bundesrat*, the upper house, is made up entirely of *Land* representatives, so the *Länder* can make their presence felt by influencing Federal legislation in the *Bundestag*, the lower house. For some legislation, agreement of the *Bundesrat* is necessary, for some not. Where it is not, the upper house can object to proposed laws, and even take matters to a conference committee where both Houses are represented and a compromise can be hammered out.

German Law is *Land*-based, with the exception of five

supreme courts and the federal constitutional court, which exists to ensure that all legislation is compatible with the Basic Law which was set up at the same time as the Republic itself.

The President of the Republic is an elected figurehead, who may serve for a maximum of two five year terms.

The system of *Länder* and central *Bund* is held in high regard throughout Germany, and *Land* politics are lively and of interest to most ordinary citizens. Many of the country's brightest and wiliest politicians are to be found at *Land* level, and have no very pressing desire to get into the Federal scene.

Bureaucracy

The Germans enjoy remorseless regulations, rigid rules. They are bound and gagged with red tape. A bureaucrat's paradise. Just as you suspected.

Crime and Punishment

It will come as no surprise that the Germans are keen on law and order. 'There must be Order' is the phrase on many a German's lips. To ensure that what must be is, the Germans are willing to sanction some fairly heavy handed policing and some very strict laws.

Adhering to rules can appear to rule out reason. A man crossed a street without waiting for the lights (it was 2 a.m. and the street was empty). Halfway across he was knocked down by a speeding car which made no attempt to avoid him. The police were called, the man put into an ambulance, and the driver was let off without a caution. Shocked, the only witness (a foreigner) asked the policeman what would happen to the injured man. He replied: "If he survives, he will pay a fine of fifty marks."

Policing is the responsibility of the various regional authorities. If you decide to make a break for it after brutally dropping your sweet wrapper in the street, and succeed in getting as far as the regional border, your case will be formally handed over to the police in the next *Land*, who will take up the chase.

The Germans must always have their identity papers with them to avoid being arrested and locked up for up to six hours while someone fetches them. If they move house, even one house further along the street, they must register their new address within a few days. No citizen can escape the long arm of the law for long.

German law can seem like a nightmare of pettiness and vindictiveness. One individual was fined because in remonstrating with a policemen he had used the word '*Mensch*', equivalent to an American saying 'Man'. No-one may imply that a policeman is a human being. Policemen are carefully vetted and if they show the tiniest sign of a sense of humour, they're out.

Law and order apply in the home too. Laws concerning noise and disturbance are rigid and, by others' standards, intrusive. Generally, all noise must cease after 10 p.m. If you live in flats, don't sing in the bath late at night, in fact, think twice about having a bath at all, and as for flushing the lavatory...

Care is needed in the sensitive matter of when you cut your lawn since doing it at weekends will probably get you into trouble, but not doing it at all will get you into worse.

The safest bet, as indicated earlier, is to assume that everything is forbidden and against the law unless you have documentary proof to the contrary (in contrast to France where everything is allowed, even if it is forbidden, and Russia where everything is forbidden, even if it is allowed).

One of the more depressing aspects of German life is that all Germans love to point out to you what you are doing wrong or what you are failing to do right. Thinking of sneaking through a red light? Don't do it. A hundred Germans will helpfully call out that This Is Not Allowed. Thinking of leaving the kids' toys out on the front lawn? Don't do it. The whole neighbourhood is itching to point out to you that This Is Not Allowed.

German rules and regulations have proliferated so much and involve such unlimited red tape that the Germans have introduced a de-bureaucratisation law to cope with them.

Business

The majority of German companies are small to medium sized, old, and family owned. The relationship between boss and employees is close and friendly. The owner usually knows precisely what goes on at shop-floor level, having worked there himself at some time.

Industrial relations have always been much better and more stable than in Britain. Bosses and unions don't necessarily admire each other, but the need for co-operation and partnership is universally recognised. In German companies everybody from the Chairman to the charlady is called a *Mitarbeiter* or co-worker, and this is not mere rhetoric. Manual workers are probably earning comparable wages to management and enjoying the same conditions and benefits (not as a privilege but as a right). More importantly, both will regard themselves as social equals.

In business, seriousness and qualifications rule the day. Amateurs won't get a look in, and specialists can get no job outside their area of expertise. If you're a Doctor of Philosophy and can't get a post in a university department, you will probably be working in a semi-skilled position. Business won't touch you with a barge pole.

Timing

At the office, punctuality is next to Godliness, although only the bosses are expected to be in early or to stay late. Most Germans knock off at 5 o'clock sharp. Working late is seen as an admission of inefficiency (which is Not Allowed), unless you choose the option to come late and leave later, or come early and leave earlier, which is known as 'gliding time'.

The Working Day

Plenty of loud grunting and complaining lets everyone know that you are exerting yourself to the utmost in the cause of *Gründlichkeit* (thoroughness). Quiet efficiency will be unnoticed by your superiors and earn you withering looks from your colleagues.

Ambition and competitiveness are the expected norm and their outward signs are intensity of effort and not sloping off every 20 minutes for a cigarette and a read of the newspaper.

Performance, skill, achievement and workmanship are all highly valued at work. If you generate a mountain of paper and memos, you are clearly working hard and good at your job.

In the old days, Germans seemed to live entirely for their work. Since finding out about foreign holidays and 101 things you can do in a tracksuit, they have become less dogged. This has led to much national anxiety and articles in *Der Spiegel* asking, 'Are We Germans Becoming Lazy?'

Occasional after-hours jollies have to be put up with, but mixing socially with your workmates is fairly uncommon. Office 'do's are pretty formal events. You are not expected to get legless and grope the canteen staff.

German business meetings stick to the agenda so as not to waste time; they therefore need extensive agendas.

Time is precious, time is money. It is not to be wasted frivolously – until someone finds the perfect opportunity to 'profile' himself and begins to hold forth on everything he knows.

Women at Work

German men have always known that German women are a force to be reckoned with. Today, business is feeling the benefit as well, as women move beyond '*Küche, Kinder, Kirche*' (kitchen, children, church).

Women make up 40% of the workforce. Germany now has more than twice as many female Members of Parliament as England, and equal opportunities and treatment for men and women are demanded in the Constitution. However, men still occupy most senior positions. Only about 2% of all top posts in industry and commerce are held by women.

Language and Ideas

In their hearts the Germans believe that no foreigner can speak German properly. (In fact, they believe that only people from their own region speak decent German. There is nothing more barbarous to a Berliner than the Bavarian version of the language. Bavarians heartily reciprocate this feeling.)

German is a remarkably flexible language, and one in which new words are easy to make up – you simply take two, three, or pretty well any number of existing ones, and stick them alltogetherabitlikethis. This doesn't just make a nice new word, it introduces a whole new concept, perhaps explaining why the German psyche is so fearfully complicated. For instance, in a park the notice *Astbruchgefahr* registers in one swift glance that you are within the orbit of 'branch-dropping-off-danger'.

An alternative to this is to take a string of words, chop out all the bits you don't care for, and glue the remainder together. This is a popular way of coping with the names of government departments and so forth – hence <u>*Staatssicher*</u> <u>*-heitsdienst*</u> (the State Security Service of the GDR).

The German printed page is startling at first. The words are so long. A newspaper article may consist of just four or five words, yet take up two columns. The same is true of sentences and paragraphs. Look at a book by Thomas Mann. A thousand pages divided into half a dozen paragraphs.

Unsurprisingly, the inventive German tongue has given rise to many ideas and notions contained in one word, which are unmatched in other languages: for example:

Realpolitik – The pursuit of political advantage or survival in a tough world. Saying, "No, really, it doesn't hurt" after your 20 stone boss has trodden on your foot.

Schadenfreude – A joy-in-destruction sort of emotion which perfectly captures the surge of satisfaction you feel on hearing of another's downfall. Other languages are very coy about honouring such a caddish feeling with a whole word of its own. Consequently, everybody uses the German one.

Weltschmerz – It's a freezing February night, the central heating has packed up, your team is facing relegation, you've just been handed your redundancy notice and arrive home to find that the dog has been sick on the sofa. The way you feel is *Weltschmerz*.

Frömmelei – The saccharine-coated piety typified by tele-evangelists who tell you that God urgently wants you to send them money, and who are subsequently found in bed with three people called Tammy (only two of whom are female). In relation to culture it describes people who have never read Shakespeare, but refer to him reverently as 'the Bard'.

Kleinkariert – This literally means having a pattern of small checks. Its proper use is to describe the sort of person who has gnomes outside their bungalow and has holidayed in Frinton for the last 25 years.

Zeitgeist – Nothing less than the Spirit of the Age, and the cue for no end of sighing and looking world-weary. An invaluable word to use whenever German cinema or the music of Stockhausen are under discussion.

Vergangenheitsbewältigung – The sum total of difficulties a nation encounters in struggling to come to terms with a dodgy past. Who but the Germans would have a word for it?

The Authors

Benjamin Nicholaus Oliver Xaver Barkow is a German of the old school. Born in Berlin in 1956, he spent his formative years lobbying to have a wall built through the city because he strongly disapproved of the way the Socialists pegged out their laundry.

With this achieved, he moved to Hamburg, but finding it such a well-ordered place, moved swiftly to London. What he found there has so appalled and fascinated him, he is unlikely ever to leave. After a tempestuous and *Angst*-ridden adolescence, he studied humanities (in the vain hope that some of it would rub off). For most of his adult life he has freelanced as a researcher and writer, and is currently writing a history of the London Wiener Library.

Despite being a chronic sufferer of *Kreislaufstörung*, which no herbal remedy has yet cured, he soldiers on in the hope that one day he will understand why people don't understand him; at which point he will take his *Seele* out of pawn, move to the mountains and begin work on his cherished project, *Wagner, the Musical*.

Stefan Zeidenitz is descended from an old German family of Anglophiles who sadly failed to catch the last Saxon long-boat to Britain by some 1½ thousand years.

He has compensated for missing the boat by immersing himself in Far Eastern studies and promoting Japanese culture in England, English culture in Germany and German culture in Japan. In consequence, his sense of direction is sometimes slightly distorted.

The effortless superiority which he encountered while teaching at St. Paul's School and Eton College has not yet superseded his Teutonic temperament. But he is working on it.